HERON/GIRLFRIEND

Also by Jen Tynes:

See Also Electric Light (Dancing Girl Press)

The Ohio System w/ Erika Howsare (Octopus Books)

The End Of Rude Handles (Red Morning Press)

Found In Nature (Horse Less Press)

HERON/GIRLFRIEND

By
Jen Tynes

Coconut Books
Atlanta, Georgia
2008

Copyright 2008 by Jen Tynes

Published by Coconut Books

www.coconutpoetry.org

All rights reserved.

ISBN: 978-0-615-25511-8

Cover Design: Meghan Punschke

Cover Art: "Exploding Brain" by Christine Hamm

Proofreaders: Nicole Cartwright Denison, Roxanne Carter, Kaya Oakes

I walk 47 miles of barbed wire,
I use a cobra-snake for a necktie,
I got a brand new house on the roadside,
Made from rattlesnake hide,
I got a brand new chimney made on top,
Made out of a human skull,
Now come on take a walk with me, Arlene,
And tell me, who do you love?

-Bo Diddley

I.

NOTA BENE

Some alien plants like hands grew out of my flowerpots.

I went to pick blackberries at the bottom of a deep bucket of grass, binded or bounding my intellectual side.

A girl who lived across the fenceline in a rented house
I plumbed, looking youthful.

She cut down some of the grasses with a short knife.

(I did not "interview" her but I have been "interviewing" her friend for six months now.)

If you think I am going to rise above something by now.

I run to eat the blackberries without dinner and leave big smashes.

If I say it will one of you say it back?

We watched a covey appear from a covey.

The largest one I ever saw was dead.

CHURCH OF STOPPING BY THE WOODS

There were no limbs.
The limbs that betray
a powerline sway-backed
or encased in blue-nosed television,

their bodies
in ice. A blank patch
where I stalled
gilded, having already

stripped and jumped over
a mother's car, children's
groceries, a thawing

hole in the pit of
white dash.
Some venison next

season, her sweetness
rang everything off
or kept the webbed

foot til it sagged.
Turned into

the dark treeline of the family
and waited for a sign:
their shuffling inside the woods

a feverish symptom
of some hard mimicry.
Held thirty seconds,

the face a whole painted body
dropping down to cover
the wreck.

Then fishing it out

full of water,
making every dim place
seem inhabitable.

GRIZZLY MAN

We watch another man's baby
climb a tree, turn
into old liquor
acorns. Describe it
like its cross-

hatched el-
bow fends, untroubled
forehead like
ear hearing early

under fog. We is the hound
and I, a heart
attack just

waiting to tell it.
Will not nothing
sustain us, a comet kind

of clean? Man in
market, braining supper.
Man in

the wilderness thinks he falls
in love with something

hairy, middle-out
of nowhere, gymnosperm,
wooden gum boots,
anything thigh-high. Quiver

apocket, something hairy off
the sideways, a burr
with something leery in

my mouth--
I make the call.

LOW-LYING

Favor some mothers
with darkened cars like
berries, turned late,

pressed hard or pulled
off a darker curb
than molding, a row

of busted headlights
tell no tales, hay
or bunting to
place some body
to the weekend,

some mother's loveseats
set back to spine,
some unlit

automobiles lining the unnerved
interstate are crystallized
deposits

inside like limbs
and weeds some contradict
when it rains
and rubs in you

some bald
spot to love,

no caravan,
procession,
some mother's

parade is gone
in the pantry,

some sibling never
learned how,
is gone in the utility

room to butcher,
will taste like
mold and some mothers

couldn't harm
a drowned bucket,
some mothers walk right

in you keep
treading into
the weekend,

back the weakened
to back the darkened
head anticipates

following, a backwards
tangle and some headlight,
mothers caught

in the folding,
dark linens
you might leave

for anytime,
a blooming

bunch some might call
cluster
or nervous

mothers leave
hanging to the
trees,

your way of burning
all night,
to let you

out of
raising some:

look several hands
above there.

CHURCH OF UNTIMELY ARTICULATION

Motioning switches   Ice holds

Banks apart a wide wet eye you would do

Whole (dirt) road taken over by your black hoop   Your black

Loop follows home it's a story under

Cross the fabric   You make face by heading or saved

The babies   Do it a row it fiddles another

Wet (hoop) eye   Y'all fall through some poses

Now seeing it

Doesn't mean as mean does   A raw pass

Than it holds more water   The crisp wall dusts

A short cut bald and low   Doesn't mean fearing

And if tire snakes   Imagine as laced

Several without coats   Bark accumulates

A severance doesn't deliver   Gathering in the thumbs

Or feel it separate   Fewer blanket and folds.

TO FIELD & STREAM

1.
Deep River
Middlesex Steam Train.

Stopped above bone
ore trees. He retreated
to the cab for it.

2.
Fishkill
Peekskill,
we crossed

the Hudson
on a fish
bridge. New Walden,
Deer

Dale Motel, Lords
Valley, Bloom

Grove, Promised
Land State
Park. My murals

can't see you
from here. Phil

Wanted, bunch
of birds on a Mobil

sign, Bellafonte.

3.
Ms. Ribs Chicken
Misread: See It Big

Bear Blooming
Grave Travelers

Delite. Motel Cocktail
Rainbow

cauls on
a line to dry.

4.
Lincoln, Nebraska
does not give me what I want--
time, temperature.

5.
      Highest
point on I
80 east
of Mississippi, pink

sloe. Levy

the watershed. A "bomb
explosion"

doesn't seem right
here.

6.

    Sun
shews the wall breaks

or brakes for
Saturn maid. Shipping

back and
forth in her cab.

7.
SPRING
township. Tiny deer

on the hill of
a roadside pulling
grass

between rocks so
small to have

antlers.

8.
Semis in velvet.

DRAUGHT

The black shape of deer with
a yellow head hangs over,
listens to

the body of my machine,
the body of my machine
repeats itself
in nature,
congresses in sessions

sideswiping it.
Captures the whites
also known as the undivided

bellies of second-growth
trees--

my machine who
howls with everyone
of its vipers, every finger

of potable liquid, every ring
around its tail,
the contraband

all stuffed in the bodies
of dogs who are waiting
at some edge of some musculature
they may not ridge.
I may not go rigid

when, impressed
upon me,

a natural configuration
blows the coop.
You see

those Canada geese.
You see the way
I pull aside.

WHEN YOU SHOVEL SNOW FROM THE SIDEWALK, CAR, WHERE DOES ALL THE SNOW GO.

The carpet takes us to heart.

The oven is a grimy pumpkin.

A squash-shaped blossom forms around one nipple like an aureole or areola.

The book that was lent us is on the shelf.
Not propping up anything--

If you are not a driver it's hard to know which way to putter.

Does it contain more than one word to say a body's halo.

You have to look when a vehicle passes, it could be your cousin.

They usually cut across the yard and pull up in here sideways.

THE CHARISMATIC WORLD

Not as precious as
these ricochets of arms
called by some
people love
taps, the action

is automatic, Hawk's wrestling
jacket slipped off
a shoulder in lieu
of safety. The reason

is because of how
the car drove past
without honking.
It follows some boys

do not know how
to skate on concrete
or ice, some force
themselves upon.
Fragmentation is

inaudible, the ocean
comes out of its element
in parcels on which straw
people learn

to string
along light.
Inside of this
opinion there is another

boat of bone. There is a similar
but bad-shaped

gymnasium, making best
of what good

egg provides.
Not as precious
as some saying.
A boat of bone

breakers beckons
the girl back
out of the man.
Watches out

for the quarter that is
fishing around them.

LAND BETWEEN THE LAKES

1.
Wet scratched
& bleeding 100

dollars of the swan.
His wife then immediately

"clobbered" him saying
it certainly hadn't been
a pleasure.

2.
Child-ducked
behind a railing,
the arresting

officer watched
half an hour

throwing a net
into Rock River,
the walleyes

& catfish
were all photographed.

3.
Three subjects

were using a seine,
a mother

had apparently
tied rope around
her son's neck,

ten subjects possession.
She then

went jet
skiing.

4.
A rural couple complained
they were awakened

one morning,
the bass boat operator

hurried away.
A boat incident

occurred near
the boat house,
caused both occupants

to be
pushed under.

5.
The subject had several
deer heads in possession,

the throttle
stuck on her
houseboat.

6.
The officers macheteed
their way
into the undergrowth.
A frozen owl

was found froze
six days later

a brand new boat.

7.
The owl was identified
their equipment included

a "Go Devil"
motor. Nothing was observed
on the river.

CHURCH OF CO' COLA

A road is jerry-
built, heaving
polished wood.
He took me in

first, the mesh
was contraband,
the firecrackers

Black Cats.
Red circles

mean think
a thing or two
about breathing.
Ladies monitor

the money-changing and circles
remain, their oak breath a tree

in the forest.
The body is a sponge

and off its rocker.
You think to lick

that fit.
Arms wrapped

of habit, that bird
knows the rounds.
Why do you think

it keeps coming
back to you?

A tie makes two
strings disappear.

NECESSARY OVERSIGHT

What honks from outside
is the evening's *safe
ride* and the water

tower that shines
in our window is
going to swerve

any second now.
Let's put on
our longjohns,
pull this off.
Wear on one
stocking each

in the mourning, matter,
our empties revisited,
you animal you.
Stand mid-road
to wait and cars

will rev against you,
burn like

better men.
Like heating up
another stranger,
emptier room.
Do not let that evening

sun go down.
Cover our covers
with the finger of
my law for you.

IT CAN BE HUSBANDED

They are parked only after the first of the blossoms

    take my grandmother's car, a red Mercury fallen from

trees blossoms in February,

    white gravel yard-singing chickens, peas the size of babies

and their branches form a vaulted white roof

              that will not alarm, considering

even a single dandelion can derail

    you from taking my grandmother's car, a red mercury will

mow down the area beneath and around the trees

                    and lie beneath me

in clusters at night.

PLAINCLOTHESED

My chaw's white
halo against this
dark slip

of road intends
to ramrod me,

you bump your
noggin against

mine, interested
in hard decisions.
I don't wanna be
your anemone

anymore, flushed
with paralysis.
Beating it

in less trafficked
spots, the bends
I jerry-rigged--

a fingertip's
decision--
that is I make

the honking with
my able hand

and later come
the geese.

II.

OF AMERICAN FORESTS

Founded upon certain wild legends I have grown both teeth and the desire to flourish.

"A certain plank-walker that would rather call this reading than learning," losing face is each separate plank mouthing off.

Do you speak with your hands or learn a trade?

Along the edges of woods, whispers about whether this can be anything other than sheer material.

Forestry, I am going flatter than a mouth-piece.

From a limited possibility mindset, I may pick at holes and hide the perennials but there is always the instinct to spring.

If you meant that, when the speakers of the houses broke into their own voices and flew away in a faction.

The darkened body of the crane is always reserving a little water.

A fallen crop in a forest is admitting he is lonely, and then they have to go and talk all over him.

ET IN THIS CENTURY

Bothered by a case
of white ones, skinbreak
out of its color into dobber-like

pearling tones. The rotary
telephone cannot be heroic, free-floating
tickets to absolute

rocking go out. If anyone becomes rabid
the locker room is painted
then relegated to wood
dowels and rubber plants, still crooked
children blow

my mind and fight with themselves.
Over shortcake's shoulder

when he still deserved
it. A concentrated watermelon
full of proof, of being

carried too far just to mumble—
if this is the gist of it—

Some girls in the "shared living
space" feeling loose in
the longjohns, epitheting back
and forth. If this is the gist of it, some boys

will set fire to small parcels
of wood and bawl
each other out for shaving.
In the corner of the corner

of what is applicable, a pineapple
crusted in its own sugars.
A wildcat is drawn
from the woods to the plastic

cups of their blouses, darkness
waves right back at you.
The muscle in charge of turning
his back upon young animals turns

the whole body against me now.
We wrangle beneath the bathroom
window and I almost swallow
my sheet.

I TOOK MY HANDS FROM THE MACHINE

Wake up feeling
like fish on
wrappers. Water that
gathers along the stitch

of the windowscreen
smells like an entire
body. Wobbles in
place. The houses of
others are seafoam

green, fingerling
yellow, batter pink.
Do you know why

that squirrel runs back
and forth across
the roof next
door? Why those
birds pick each
other on the spot?
In the morning I will go

back to my country
and pick up all
the manuals, will turn
right back around

when the road devolves
into allegation. All the dead
raccoons en route

were once ghosts
in the machinery like us,
then they accepted
their serious wardrobes.

HE NAMES ALL THE HORSES AFTER HER

Against the fence nests
of yellowjackets and field
rabbits I carry home stunned
and smelling sheltered--
baked too long, stunned. Too late
in the day to water, we leave her alone
with her daylilies, forget-
me-nots and soap
operas. Too late in the day
for fishing but he draws back
the barbed-wires I pass under
and we follow the fences, erratic, taking
an acre now and again and fighting
over them in the evening. (*They throw head-
lit punches against the crooked tree
line.*) The honeysuckled gap
the horse pressed and stepped over
is still buzzing, shot
and later that dusk the glass door
between us he will chase her around
the house her hooves deep in tulip
beds darkly flashing a throat
of pearls her iron
sloppy cool and ringing across
the tangle of stepping stones
and garbage sack bottoms he buried
in the garden himself.

BETTER TO SITE IT

I fell all over myself
in 'some dark holler,' no sense
of the beds that deer have
made. Myself preparing to lie

flat in the grass play
stupid for the piddlingest
deputy. I love a bit of shine

on my circumstance,
for the sake of conservation
if your chest has its own
medal and affords

a Buick stretched out
in front of me, I am happy

to stay coiled in my bushel
or harvest. At the bottom of both
season and valley there's
a citronella safety

net, an antiseptic bath.
The little light that bows
from someone else's concrete
entry-way. Already the peastone

has migrated into the mowed
areas, making problematic
music come out of the machines.
At night I sugar forth

like a home-owner again blip
blipping my secret code.

FACT-FINDING

After your own,
the heat generated
by small engines in
small power

tools. The first
true animal
comes out

of a wobble,
another pink skin
flint needling
its face up

into my face.
Where I drive
each day is a gift
I am taking

to heart without
apologizing
for pausing.

So where does
every heat exit.

A MYTH

My love may make your skin
turn red and raw: turn into
some ashes, my love might give
you tremens if you can call that
out and make it likened to

a sound: my body, a rough
instrument or a roughly planted
bundle of flowers, a black grecian
sentiment that starts with
O! If I were a man instead

of a bear I would celebrate the way
that you move on to a different
thought when we are talking
in the afternoon in the front yard
in front of everybody: the body

turns to perfect glass: the body of the city
we are loving each other through
is the sort of thing that goes

transparent when you start thinking

about it: something else entirely

is about to stop our hearts. Think about

the taste of river water. Don't come up

on me from behind and present

that as a transformation.

I know you are neither angelic

nor inanimate, I am nothing

but a bear who wants to make things

glimmer with my muzzle

tucked into the water, tipped

down into the water and back:

up to find the roseate

glow of your black

old border: everyone else has left

us alone on the grass by

the patches of hard-dropped peonies,

and it is almost going

to be morning.

YOU ARE TALL AND WELL SET UP

[   ]
I fell in with you were already married I took to bottling calves

[   ]
Meat shed steam shed rock shed weed shed pump shed runts so smother

[   ]
Half-buried machinery sometimes a joke cut short the space a blessing

[   ]
You cleared the frogs the coons the strays the owls so only one

[   ]
Choose to sit this evening out then horses' muscles kick

[   ]
Dove-tail dovecote dome of niches you make your cleft a figure

[   ]
Is not saying how you want to croak kick the lantern lose it all

[   ]
Even pinned up under porches all the dogs get weird

[   ]
Clot over gratings silent empty we aren't splitting another

[   ]
Still won't float a wolf a fowl a knobby bag of grain

[   ]
Levered moorings thumbs twice-over soaking steam the windows

[   ]
Make a list and button my lips split rabbit on thin ice

HERON/GIRLFRIEND

Evening I cut everything down
its middle. Round from working places
instead of self. Figurines
slipped off their mantels,
and other animals

stay on like the dark,
drawing it.
We have nets
and boxes and we eat

on the quarter hour and sleep
with each other.
You don't speak any language
I understand, your know-how calls

for it and it comes crashing
into single-leggedness.
I am flat as the carnival

and can't let it lie,
talk to the oven
with every hand
available, ambient.
For now trees keep

outside the house,
you haven't carried them
into pieces. You glass
transformer.
Mocking bird.

LEGHORN

I'm real buddy-buddy with the multiple

inlets, the hawks that, although

they are ominous, bury their children

in bouquets. "Natural" bridges don't

horrify easily—the girl inside the toll

booth beneath the bridge is a killer

but no one will make the call. Pretend

I am not in the back of your compact

and tell her what you are thinking:

about the migration of Canada geese

there is another kind of opening.

THE ARBITRAGE

Equinox

Into chairs a visionary inability
aligning shoulders hips everything
is special repeats represents or counts
them on her hands
and knees their word deer
for dinner or pullet instead skyblue
size of his thumb but not
from there fingers can't
touch still guides
the guide.

Muffler

Take what you want
from desire and turn
over this fits
my system the doting smells
of cabinets somehow my hair's
held back mercury to bulb we roll
with it this is all
the daylight all
the spoons in your mouth
all new all suffered your hands feel
like ice.

Vertigo

That step was affected not on top
of images pictures of pictures
not filibuster
the divorce with meaning

bring us some
sandwiches it's raining
this time it's a euphemism
for keel the queen anne etc
only has three legs you hide
it well.

Moderate

They get tired
of the ocean when they get tired
of the ocean and the fact
they juggle horseshoes they do it
bareback they build
a barn burn sometimes
they dream of whaling they whale
and whale and whale.

Sesame

Three dogs buried but still
the brown carpet she laughs
her ass off white
bellied like dinner coyote
at the door these are just
things call it
local flavor call
and call it
won't come.

WOOF AT THE DOOR

Look at these girls!
Every one is my cousin!
I changed their diapers into dumpheaps
and look at them now!
They have bosoms and blonde hair the color
of steel!
As babies, their blonde hair

and bare chests were the color of corn
and mercury!
They were tobacco princesses, husk
queens then!

SOME MAIDENHEADS ARE VETTED

Come to town on the backs
of some relatives-scorned,
I can get me

some of my own
supper anyway.
Treading

within an inch of pot-
belly blackness.
The belle of this woods

is hair-kneed,
a white elephant
hunting a lyre.

Tail tucked,
gone hamper-

fishing, men on
the river know not

what we do.
The bodies we muck
through, hunting

a liar. I am tarred
of taling you
all night long.

I have my own
fur weakness.

CHURCH OF THUNDEROUS APPLAUSE

Shared my beard with company and look where it got me.
A night you fight makes waste.

You are better to stand in the bushes, crying out.
You only have one hand.

A proverb smokes its stacks, burns autumn leaves taut.
Why don't we have children, would they make a face?

Everyone at the party was open-mouthed except the children.
I placed us outside them and I became afraid.

I love walking in the clipped evening my pantlegs all burred.
I can't remember what you said you cut.

Is the man in the moon being simple?
A hand is in my mouth making teeth.

THE JACKAL GRANDFATHER

Bone doesn't light the mouth
of the cave, catch fish
because I told you to,
sleep late

into the evening
and when someone
isn't looking

smart leave
fingerprints
to guide us after.

Switching his boots
is a joke, the jacket

still bears
an emblem,
the cabinet has

a family.
Barriers on

the river don't
say anything
new, don't stay

anything slipped
loose by those
dogs of ours.

THE PRESERVATION

No one else should be watching
the dam empty Lake Barkley Christmas
morning but another car
also sits the levee. Its diligent windows

of jagged frost make us look
away and away from each other:
the junked floorboard, our webbed fingers
after centuries of twiddling,
white sky between them

white rolling til it breaks.
It is about to snow.
We will leave

some self beneath the ice to swallow,
some one to watch the floodgates turn.

AN OPEN FIELD

□

I am saying
I was shy about saving grace
with my hands. Junket and

junket is expanding--
found out, even. Smell of hot
radio. Something about

kingdoms. I always felt old, violent
or whatever. We drink

to each other without
listening. The evergreen does

screen it.

□

You wet tree for them. I know
declarations--

seasonal humor is an animal
this morning. I had a drink of water

in the back of my mind.
And all the lights that say

I will not miss this hissing
pair in the back.

□

I guess this is all the evening

comes from. The open air, the stairs
for watching smoke.

A dog for too many
seasons. Everyone's name

on the ground, on the edge
of rising up.

I need to stop our house.

□

Sits without people at this
morning. Wasn't

heavy stone. If this
table catches

no wind the burning
smells can't remember.

You call me into the water.

◻

Up in some trees, the tangle.
We sever in clumps all over

soon, like heroes.
On the coast they hope

about aliens but still

change clothes and continue.
Not akin to talking,
same place.

◻

Do we ask for cords of wood?
This morning a wild

frame within me. Neither being one
nor direct movement makes people.

Let slip the mouths
of hearth and kin.

.

DARKNESS CREEPS UPON US

Everything, even our family's speech,
has a hole in it that must be tamped
with absolute electricity. Primitivism
is a loaded, gum-filled mouth in
my eyes. I see mechanisms coming
to each other. There are only windows
to the soul and windows looking
out of it, into other windows lighted
because it is dark outside. What kind
of friend recognizes their enemies.
Another kind of saying will take you out
of aphorism's hand, another kind leads
all sounds back into the forest, nicking
the ground's small lantern. Absolute
statements are uneconomical, make us
sorry in the eyes of the law— for every
glowing latitude a city,
a citizen. Let any other
animal feed this homily.

SOME PROMISE

I don't know about you but my skin
when it hallows is nothing like
an anvil, when I strike the anvil
it sounds nothing like

a bell. I live in a stained-
glass house with my wife
and all her children. We only run
ragged, milky animals too late

at night or first thing
in the morning, when the paper
doesn't come. In the green room
and yellow field of warning

I like to translate everything
my son, the figurative, will need
to make it home. To my daughter

the material, I wriggle
the superior bait, god's live
wire. An animal

meat gone deep
and dark after crossing it
with everything twice.

REDLIGHT LAMPLIGHT

Pretend I'm the one that brung you
here and kick all else like a danger.
In the natural world, colors slip
off to "disremember," grow
poisonous in the backs
of cars. The place I'm from dangles
in a home-made mosquito
light, and every girl camps
evenings in her own wet halo.
In the natural world, suits slouch
off themselves, children go to
the Jungle Room to skunk
the way of dreams.
When we get too far gone
I am going to swing you.
You are going to let me.

III.

FRESH WITH ME

Everything is hot when taken
out of the body and into town.
We find a little piece of snake
dried up in the bricks' lab-
yrinth, white iron
roses wrought into relatives'
skin. In back of the hobbled red
wagon two babies smoke thinly,
pinch their fingers in brass wing-
like hinges. You can interfere
with yourself in the hallway's
glass but like everything, I will be
bothered. When you remove
the epithet from its hidey hole
and you are facing God all
the sudden? He uses the pidgin
reserved for punishment,
what we know plus everything
he has been thinking about us.

THE DELIVERY

My deliberate father has thrown a pencil jar across a room, an actual jelly jar full of pencils.

My actual father has not eaten clams and does not consider doing so.

My clairvoyant father sows.

Father has dated a girl out of high school, think of the long white sides of any house.

My dormer windows shutter.

My dedicated father longing for apples, his collar soon soaked.

When my ostentatious father comes calling the doors of Wal-Mart are always open, it is a twenty-four-hour store now.

My onward father, the buffalo.

My sexual father and I go rafting and buy a hunting bunting, a very warm rabbit.

My sense is such that when my delicate father falls there are onions on his breath.

My fog-headed father is cleaning out the fish tanks like a field mouse does.

My trepidatious father was swarthy in his choice of words, the evening started with a rope.

My understanding of my doddering father is the sound I make when I doll myself up.

My mistreated father says what.

My saccharine father and I, we don't talk much about television, we just watch it with the sound turned on.

My dutiful father has been neighbor to known animals.

They are facing each other across the barren field.

Or, my father stays in another room, hanging by the end of his thread.

My derisible father once took us halfway to the moon before we realized we'd plumb forgotten our sandbags and gripping gloves back down on earth.

My thick father stomping, make the world go away.

I do not preface any of my loves.

My wild ideas about my father devolve into nausea, knack of being the real king of kings, orphans in their own hearts.

My perishable father does not know how to call a cab.

My delivery might be lacking but my figurative father is laughing in the face of bankruptcy.

My father is at home.

My contestable father had both his eyes replaced and his back made out of soda cans, a real mean machine.

My illiterate father makes me bees.

My allocation of fatherhood is based on a tenderness I feel upon taking the last dusty Mountain Dew can from the corner of the fridge.

Without asking, my starved father and I make a conversation out of wings, backs, and neck bones.

A palatable section of chicken feed is dried and gathered by my very own father in spite of his loneliness.

If a finger were to materialize from the countryside and point me all the way over.

My applicable father in one hand while the other one turns over.

Go out to the timber and find my father in a flock of merciful birds.

A GRASS WIDOW

Full of fiber in a Halloween field
where I stumped and harangued
it to shreds. When it is your own
hand you make a bee-line, bird-
like, into the civilized zone. Back
yard will, if you let it, fill itself
with the open mouth of you, spook
another living thing or two, preclude
ID. When I call upon the second
person in the atonal point-
of-view, you can imagine
our rooms.

A HIGHRISE FOR THE ELDERLY IS LIKE A DAMP QUARTERED BIRD

A highrise for the elderly is like
a damp quartered bird,
fire-proofed but not
a story. Technical

wiring in the openings,
on Sundays fuses busted when
the elderly make some
stew, the light plates

are kicked offward.
The elderly are kicking things
like horses in
the sides, riding

off on the backs
of pitted, frozen latkes. Where
will we put our stirring
spoons in, where

will we darken
the door just a little
to keep it from knocking
around.

AN INDEPENDENT VIEW OF THE INSTITUTION

I am not writing one of those poems:
our neighbor is a construction
worker who bangs

his palm on the roof
of passing cars.
I am not winging

it with Superman: though
he may be unlike
most people he is nothing

unlike me. I do not turn
on the bathroom
like an animal,
with poverty

feelers, drain pipe
organs, biography.
Whatever I tell you

it is just
on the telephone.
When my head hits
the pillow I cannot say:

I do not know
how to make this, stranger.

SOUND WAVES, LASER BEAMS, IMPULSES AND SIGNALS

I feel like a mother when I wear some
one else's shoes, when I tie someone else's
laces into rabbit's foot darkness
at dawn, the mailman coming and rubbing
my heels together, to go home. I feel
like a mother talking loudly around
young boys and their fragrant tufts
of armpit hair on the subway,
revving my engine on the highway,
in the yard, and when I am not behind
the wheel making horn noises with my
nose and mouth. Somewhere a mother
has forgotten how to breathe water,
insists that everyone ought to be breathing
air by now. I feel like a mother when
my mother is dead although it hasn't happened
yet that I feel like a motherless child.
When I list the names
of my enemies in the free grocery
bulletin, the T's growing a long
moustache. I feel like a mother
when I shave my beard and all
my children tiptoe around us giggling
from their blades. When I am offered
glasses of wine without pieces of bread
soaking in them, when I transmit my own
signals from antennas in a jar
of the earth to a cage full of animals
in the livingroom. I feel like a mother
for cooking those books
for you but that wasn't love
it was history.

ATTENTION CANINE

All my boyfriends get it
in the ribs now and then,
the rumored fifth season
vanished when it pulled
off-road. My position is
strictly "Rock On Palm,"
my sign the gravel-
spangled anti-mega-hog.
The dark little bulb
around the dotted eyes
tries to go "country," only
to connect to thin line, but
we cannot predict whether
weather sticks. The hogs pop
one another inside their
troughs. I sat there where
her seat used to be and
didn't get all mouthy.
The ivory fist fights
you are dreaming about,
the autumn teeth falling
out there aren't mine.

THE STAFF

Bark is removed from
its body which shops all
over town for shoulders
of lamb. Lights take a couple
back there. Meat is bright when
it can't cash checks fashioned
out of it, pearly burdens that
bric-a-brac but don't spoil this
for me. Rod is forever buried
to his nose in a couple of jokers,
is called a cigarillo in the lake
area, where lips are inlets. Only
company rips along its tendons
and lies down, a sloping hillside
staff accepts for exercise. Monster-
mashed in the closet together,
bodies with dogs attached to go
along with blood, lust, sticks or
carrots--comfort me when
you cannot break for lunch.

GIVE ME A FOOT

I am every honcho
in the moment
of realizing Fay

Wray's love,
breaking over
barstools more
intricate barstools

getting to the gist
of prehistory.
Before I was able

to tell you
a story I was
definitely

a manly girdle, an eater
of figurative
language.

I gave rabies
to myself in the middle
of the ocean,

I stopped short
of dyeing
it red. That kind

of line break--
stereotypical

bush, as in
ambush.
I rolled
up my sleeves,
delivered

brunches to
the boys.
Like all the sexes
I could not spell

mimosa but I went
unearthly,
stopped making
its noises out.
I shaved

the pan cake,
I cut out all
the pace.
The appeal

of a riddle is
not lost
on me.

Silence during
previews.

A BIG DEAL THING

I have touched the little Trevors
and Williamses of the map, uncrumpled
the work we did yesterday and found it
soft and incomplete. Like ball players
palm, like lovers do, scratched jewel
cases stick to their stories and bend
a dollar bill backwards. If I am too explicit
harbor me on someone else's lawn, grass
stain making a power playful. Is astronomer
weed, architectural blade, is the blue-
gray cover of physicians? If I am abetting
"knowing" looks like fuel.
If you are ready to take
the car, you'll have to
back it out of me.

FORESHADOW

I am the airport shuttle
service which is just

like being the airport itself
but a far cry from being one
of its airplanes. I have raised

ugly children up out of
my temperament and into
hardened darts, fallen

and landed right beside
me, anticipating
everything and still

gasping with one hand.
I have made my body

a row of tall, white
men on vacation, in walking
shorts I have cut them

off from the largest, most heathery
fields where the rest of the family

jumbles into one
another. I have made a path

for us and made us
sit down saying,
sadly--look at
the sour hairiness

of our needs.
Can we never burst

SCHOOL

Lots of women look like madonnas without having
learned to forgive,
                        or because I walk behind you
quickly with ball bearings inside. There
are girls in long skirts and mallets, wickets
or some other instrument
of war-pleasure in the field
where we sit and wait
for a bus to pick us up.
                        Or anyone else who dropped
the ball the way we have, kept all their keys
in one tough egg that hatches
in a pocket and announces you before you
are ready to tell a girl a thing or two
about finishing things.
                        Or a car honks at it instead
of your body. Or you
are what puts the gasoline in all
the automobiles of the world.

SUSPENSION

I am an attack
on the whole green
ocean, disguised
as a bridge in decline.
I take the entire space

allowed to me splaying fifty
rosebud toenails forty

feet like birds. Like birds we have tried
planting a giant eye on me--

from the outside it looks
like netting. Everyone looks
into my hollow and hollers
their own names.
I give holy hell
back in pieces.

SO MUCH DEPENDS

The FBI is big-hearted and blowsy in
the morning, its underwear
crying uncle from the Appalachian clothes-

line. Everything is a wire
when you are waking up,
the bosom rises artificially
and floods the archipelago or
you "levee" it in song.
Dark parameters
of the soul catch

your mother with a stranger,
                              light her
hurricane lamp. Is disaster a naturalistic
mnemonic device? Even the fuzz
won't hang around after breakfast.
                                      The parking lot
windows fog because
this is where you live.
                        Nobody left standing
this long could recall
the particulars: a heat set
upon us, a little red
chicken, the vicinity
riveting off.

ALL THE CROSS-EYED COWBOYS WILL BE LONELY TONIGHT

As if I shot too many moons
last night, I eat cantaloupe
straight from its tube and
think about your Samsonite
locks. Everything I own
is in some bag beside some
door. Everything I eat turns
my heart into unharvested
wool, a ba-boom! you fall
asleep on.

I HAVE BEEN HAVING SEX DREAMS ABOUT EVERYONE

                    Even behind
the wheel of my own car. Sisters jump
out many-armed like teenagers,
talking about hitching to Indiana
and the big theatres there. Slipping
in a puddle over
and over, bait smeared on the back
of my hand like the deep sienna
of love. On the way inside, where
another bunch of old federal
friends dance on or in stages
like strangers. Who is this wrong
geezer in his half-darkened
cabinette on the ocean, a pair of ballerina
slippers slung over the handles
of his fiery furnace? A football star bright
and blankly hanging in the night
sky when we walk out to the grove
to do our business. I am repositioning
your spinal column, I am making you
one more deal. If you are reading
this I am shaking
your shoulder in the back
of a van, a parking lot, several
hours before our flight will land.
I am telling you for once, it has started
to snow in the hinterlands.

TAKING UP WITH YOU

A sawhorse in the dark side-
yard worries us about death
in several wooden languages.
We fall sunning and stunning into
the hallowed patches below titled
mountains. Here at sea-level, blades
whistle lamely against each
other, fire ants burn in
their own shadows. Lipstick
on the teeth makes a story
run especially long and loose-
ended, though I can't say more
specifically why. The compromise
you make for living inside of
sin sings, people chain themselves
to the rough trunk of your pledge.

WHAT YOU ARE WITNESSING

I am not the plaintive
until I make the plaintive
cry, a place-

holding sound. If you are only
listening to me you cannot
tell if I am talking

about the person you remember
from the waterworks—green tie, full
of consideration: he stands
to the side when he draws
his little box elder hedges out
of nothing. You cannot tell

anyone apart from what they wear,
those big bottleneck suits.
In the courtroom everyone is big-
boned and facile according
to how they was
raised. I would pull

you out of the forgiving
earth if I thought
you could tell me what goes
on down there, but you are like everyone,

unsure how to die. The defendant only thinks
of the other orange Honda, how the sunlight
finally made it open up.

DROUGHT

The warp of a second wind
tells me to get in there and dig
a trench out of you; this is not wrong-
headed. Think

of all the prehistoric
people in their fields, judicious
and kind in the way
they choose not

to verbalize our shortcomings.
They have gone so many days
without even the idea
of rain, and we too

do not deliver.
We have the largest bodies
in this fossil bed.
If someone does not make a call

before they close up shop
for the night, all will settle
around a mouth that does not
cry and branches
that cannot leave--

in the morning they will be calling
something long and burdened
by our name.

ACKNOWLEDGEMENTS

Thanks to the following publications, where these poems (some in different form) have appeared:

"Nota Bene" in TYPO; "Church of Stopping by the Woods," "Church of Co' Cola," and "Church of Thunderous Applause" in GUTCULT; "Low-Lying" and "The Arbitrage" in OCTOPUS; "To Field & Stream," "An Open Field," and "Land Between the Lakes" in THE CULTURAL SOCIETY; "Draught," "A Myth," "A Highrise for the Elderly is Like a Damp Quartered Bird," "What You Are Witnessing," and "Sound Waves, Laser Beams, Impulses and Signals" in NO TELL MOTEL; "Redlight Lamplight" in THE BEDSIDE GUIDE TO NO TELL MOTEL: SECOND FLOOR; "When You Shovel Snow.." and "Of American Forests" in CAN WE HAVE OUR BALL BACK; "He Names All The Horses After Her" in NEW HAMPSHIRE REVIEW; "Better to Site It," "Some Maidenheads are Vetted," and "Et in This Century" in LIT; "The Eleanor Roosevelt" and "Necessary Oversight" in COCONUT; "Plainclothesed," "I Took My Hands From The Machine," and "Heron/Girlfriend" in SALTGRASS; "Fact-Finding" in SEE ALSO ELECTRIC LIGHT, a chapbook by DANCING GIRL PRESS; "The Charismatic World" in CELLAR DOOR; "It Can Be Husbanded" and "Your are Tall and Well Set Up" in AUFGABE; "Leghorn" and "Church of Untimely Articulation" in DENVER QUARTERLY; "Some Promise" in 42OPUS, "The Delivery" in LA PETITE ZINE; "Grass Widow," "The Staff," "A Big Deal Thing," "So Much Depends," "Drought," and "Taking up with You" in MELANCHOLIA'S TREMULOUS DREADLOCKS; "Right to Privacy" and "An Independent View of the Institution" in CANNIBAL; "Give Me a Foot" in a limited-edition tinyside from BIG GAME BOOKS; "School" and "Foreshadow" in STIMULUS RESPOND; and "Suspension" in THE HAT.

THANK YOU Conan Kelly, Monica Berlin, C.D. Wright, Keith Waldrop, Rosmarie Waldrop, Erika Howsare, Tyler Carter, Adam Tobin, Jibade-Khalil Huffman, Kate Schapira, Caroline Whitbeck, Bronwen Tate, Lynn Xu, Tod Edgerton, Bruce Covey, Meghan Punschke, Christine Hamm, Kate Greenstreet, Nicole Cartwright Denison, Roxanne Carter, Kaya Oakes, RISCA, "some others," not-too-gentle readers and writers.

This activity is made possible in part by a grant from the Rhode Island State Council on the Arts, through an appropriation by the Rhode Island General Assembly and a grant from the National Endowment for the Arts.

ABOUT THE AUTHOR

Jen Tynes lives in Denver, Colorado, with her husband Conan Kelly. She has also lived in Kentucky, Georgia, Texas, Illinois, and Rhode Island. With Erika Howsare she edits *Horse Less Press*.

www.ingramcontent.com/pod-product-compliance
Lightning Source LLC
Chambersburg PA
CBHW031208090426
42736CB00009B/826